RENNES TRAVEL GUIDE 2024

Exciting Things To Do In Rennes

Bonita Green

Copyright © [2024] [Bonita Green]

All rights reserved.

No part of this publication may be reproduced, distributed, or transmitted in any form or by any means, including photocopying, recording, or other electronic or mechanical methods, without the prior written permission of the publisher, except in the case of brief quotations embodied in critical reviews and certain other noncommercial uses permitted by copyright law.

Table of content

Introduction	4
Welcome to Rennes	4
Brief History of Rennes	8
Why Visit Rennes?	13
Chapter One: Getting to Know Rennes	20
Geography and Climate	20
Culture and Language	24
Local Cuisine and Culinary Delights	29
Chapter Two: Exploring Rennes City Center	34
Historic Landmarks and Monuments	34
Vibrant Markets and Shopping Districts	39
Cultural Institutions and Museums	44
Chapter Three: Discovering the Surrounding Areas	50
Day Trips from Rennes	50
Charming Villages and Towns Nearby	61
Chapter Four: Experiencing Rennes Nightlife and Entertainment	67
Bars, Pubs, and Nightclubs	67
Live Music and Performance Venues	72
Festivals and Events Calendar	77
Chapter Five: Practical Information and Travel Tips	86
Accommodation Options and Recommendations	86

Transportation Guide: Getting Around Rennes	92
Safety Tips and Emergency Contacts	98
Conclusion	105
Final Thoughts on Rennes	105
Recap of Must-See Attractions and Activities	109
Farewell and Bon Voyage	114
Travel Planner	118

Introduction

Welcome to Rennes

Rennes, the capital city of the Brittany region in northwestern France, welcomes visitors with its rich history, vibrant culture, and charming ambiance. Situated on the banks of the Ille and Vilaine rivers, Rennes is a city that seamlessly blends its medieval heritage with modernity, offering a plethora of attractions and experiences for travelers to explore.

Geography and Climate:

Rennes is located approximately 350 kilometers southwest of Paris, making it easily accessible by various means of transportation, including train, bus, and car.

The city is characterized by its picturesque landscape, with lush greenery, winding rivers, and historic architecture defining its unique charm.

The climate in Rennes is temperate oceanic, with mild summers and cool winters. Average temperatures range from around 3°C (37°F) in January to 19°C (66°F) in July, making it an ideal destination to visit year-round. However, visitors should be prepared for occasional rainfall, particularly in the autumn and winter months.

Culture and Language:

Rennes boasts a rich cultural heritage, influenced by its Celtic roots and Breton traditions. The city is renowned for its vibrant arts scene, with numerous theaters, galleries, and music venues showcasing local talent and international performances alike.

The Breton language, alongside French, is still spoken and celebrated in Rennes, adding to the city's cultural diversity and sense of identity. While French is the primary language used for communication, visitors may encounter signs, street names, and festivals in Breton, providing a glimpse into the region's linguistic heritage.

Local Cuisine and Culinary Delights:

No visit to Rennes would be complete without indulging in its delectable culinary offerings. From traditional Breton crepes and galettes to fresh seafood sourced from the nearby coast, the city boasts a diverse array of gastronomic delights to tantalize the taste buds of visitors.

Local markets, such as the Marché des Lices, offer a feast for the senses, with stalls brimming with farm-fresh produce, artisanal cheeses, and aromatic spices. Meanwhile, quaint cafes and Michelin-starred restaurants dot the cityscape, inviting visitors to savor the flavors of Brittany in a relaxed and convivial atmosphere.

Whether you're exploring the historic city center, embarking on a culinary adventure, or immersing yourself in the local culture, Rennes offers a warm welcome to all who venture to discover its many treasures. With its captivating blend of old-world charm and contemporary vibrancy, Rennes is sure to leave a lasting impression on every traveler who sets foot in this enchanting city.

Brief History of Rennes

Rennes, the capital city of the Brittany region in northwestern France, boasts a rich and storied history that spans over two millennia. From its humble beginnings as a Gallic settlement to its modern-day status as a thriving cultural and economic hub, Rennes has witnessed centuries of evolution, conquests, and revolutions that have shaped its identity and landscape.

Early Settlements and Roman Influence (circa 2nd century BCE - 5th century CE): The origins of Rennes can be traced back to pre-Roman times when it was inhabited by the Gauls, a Celtic tribe known as the Redones. The settlement, known as Condate, flourished as a trading center and military outpost due to its strategic location along the Condate Riedonum, an ancient Roman road.

During the Roman conquest of Gaul in the 1st century BCE, Condate came under Roman control and was renamed Ratumacos. The Romans left their mark on the city with the construction of roads, bridges, and defensive walls, laying the foundation for its future growth and prosperity.

Medieval Era and Breton Domination (5th century - 15th century):

Following the fall of the Western Roman Empire in the 5th century, Rennes became part of the Kingdom of Brittany, a Celtic realm established by migrating Britons fleeing Anglo-Saxon invasions in Britain. Under Breton rule, Rennes flourished as a center of trade, culture, and learning, with the construction of churches, monasteries, and fortifications shaping its medieval skyline.

The city experienced periods of prosperity and turmoil, as rival factions vied for power and influence. In the 14th and 15th centuries, Rennes emerged as a key player in the Breton War of Succession, a conflict between rival claimants to the Duchy of Brittany. The city's allegiance shifted between the French monarchy and the Breton dukes, ultimately leading to its incorporation into the Kingdom of France in 1532.

Renaissance and Enlightenment (16th century - 18th century):

During the Renaissance period, Rennes experienced a cultural and architectural renaissance, with the construction of grand mansions, palaces, and public buildings that reflected the city's newfound prosperity and prestige. The arrival of the printing press in the 16th century spurred intellectual and artistic endeavors, cementing Rennes' reputation as a center of learning and innovation.

The Enlightenment brought further advancements in science, philosophy, and politics, as Rennes emerged as a hotbed of intellectual activity and political debate. The city played a prominent role in the French Revolution, with revolutionary fervor sweeping through its streets and squares, leading to the overthrow of the monarchy and the establishment of the First French Republic in 1792.

Modernization and Urban Development (19th century - present):

The 19th century marked a period of rapid industrialization and urbanization for Rennes, as the city expanded beyond its medieval walls to accommodate a growing population and economy. The construction of railways, canals, and factories fueled economic growth, while urban renewal projects transformed the cityscape with wide boulevards, parks, and public squares.

In the 20th century, Rennes emerged as a major administrative, educational, and cultural center, with the establishment of universities, research institutes, and government institutions. The city's economy diversified with the growth of industries such as technology, healthcare, and tourism, cementing its reputation as a dynamic and forward-thinking metropolis.

Today, Rennes stands as a vibrant and cosmopolitan city, where centuries of history and heritage intersect with modern innovation and creativity. From its ancient Roman ruins to its bustling city center, Rennes invites visitors to embark on a journey through time, exploring the many layers of its fascinating past and promising future.

Why Visit Rennes?

Rennes, the capital city of the Brittany region in northwestern France, offers visitors a captivating blend of history, culture, and natural beauty that makes it a must-visit destination. From its medieval streets and historic landmarks to its vibrant arts scene and culinary delights, Rennes has something to offer every traveler. Here are several compelling reasons why you should consider adding Rennes to your travel itinerary:

Rich Cultural Heritage:

Rennes boasts a rich cultural heritage that is evident in its historic architecture, museums, and cultural institutions. The city's medieval old town, with its cobblestone streets and timber-framed houses, provides a picturesque backdrop for exploring centuries of history and heritage. Visitors can wander through the winding alleyways of the Saint-Malo district, admire the grandeur of the Rennes Cathedral, or explore the remains of the ancient Roman city walls.

Vibrant Arts Scene:

Rennes is home to a thriving arts scene, with numerous galleries, theaters, and performance venues showcasing local and international talent. The city's contemporary art center, the Frac Bretagne, hosts rotating exhibitions of modern art, while the Opera de Rennes presents a diverse program of opera, ballet, and classical music performances. Street art enthusiasts will also appreciate the vibrant murals and graffiti scattered throughout the city, adding a colorful touch to its urban landscape.

Culinary Delights:

Food lovers will delight in Rennes' culinary offerings, which draw inspiration from both traditional Breton cuisine and international influences. Visitors can sample local specialties such as savory crepes, buttery pastries, and fresh seafood sourced from the nearby coast. The city's bustling markets, such as the Marché des Lices, offer a feast for the senses, with stalls selling farm-fresh produce, artisanal cheeses, and regional delicacies. Meanwhile, cozy bistros and gourmet restaurants serve up innovative takes on classic dishes, showcasing the best of Brittany's culinary heritage.

Natural Beauty and Outdoor Activities:

Surrounded by lush countryside and picturesque landscapes, Rennes offers ample opportunities for outdoor exploration and recreation. The nearby Brocéliande Forest, steeped in Arthurian legend, beckons hikers and nature enthusiasts with its ancient woodlands and scenic trails. The Vilaine River, which winds its way through the city, provides the perfect setting for boating, kayaking, and picnicking along its banks. In the summer months, visitors can escape the hustle and bustle of the city and relax at one of Rennes' many parks and gardens, such as the Parc du Thabor or the Jardin du Palais Saint-Georges.

Dynamic Urban Culture:

As a university city and regional hub, Rennes pulsates with energy and creativity, offering a dynamic mix of nightlife, shopping, and cultural events. The city's youthful population infuses its streets with a vibrant atmosphere, particularly in the lively student quarter around Place Sainte-Anne. Visitors can browse the eclectic boutiques and artisanal shops that line the Rue Saint-Michel, sample local craft beers at cozy pubs and microbreweries, or dance the night away at one of Rennes' many bars and nightclubs.

In conclusion, Rennes offers a unique and unforgettable travel experience, with its rich cultural heritage, vibrant arts scene, culinary delights, and natural beauty inviting visitors to explore and discover all that this enchanting city has to offer. Whether you're a history buff, an art aficionado, a foodie, or simply seeking adventure, Rennes promises to captivate and inspire you with its myriad charms.

19

Chapter One: Getting to Know Rennes

Geography and Climate

Its strategic location, approximately 350 kilometers southwest of Paris, positions it as a gateway to the stunning natural beauty and cultural riches of Brittany.

Geography:

The city of Rennes spans an area of approximately 50 square kilometers, encompassing a mix of urban, suburban, and rural landscapes. Its historic city center, known as the "Ville Intra-Muros," is surrounded by 18th-century defensive walls, which enclose a maze of narrow streets, charming squares, and architectural treasures dating back centuries.

Beyond the city center, Rennes extends into modern neighborhoods and industrial zones, where contemporary architecture and infrastructure blend seamlessly with the surrounding countryside. The outskirts of the city are dotted with picturesque villages, sprawling parks, and agricultural fields, offering residents and visitors alike a peaceful retreat from the hustle and bustle of urban life.

Climate:

Rennes experiences a temperate oceanic climate, characterized by mild summers, cool winters, and moderate rainfall throughout the year. The city enjoys four distinct seasons, each bringing its own unique charm and opportunities for outdoor activities.

Summer (June - August) in Rennes is warm and pleasant, with average temperatures ranging from 15°C to 25°C (59°F to 77°F). It is the perfect time to explore the city's parks and gardens, take leisurely walks along the riverbanks, or enjoy outdoor festivals and events.

Autumn (September - November) brings cooler temperatures and vibrant foliage, as the surrounding countryside bursts into a kaleidoscope of reds, oranges, and yellows. Visitors can immerse themselves in the beauty of the changing seasons by hiking through nearby forests, sampling seasonal produce at local markets, or attending cultural performances and exhibitions.

Winter (December - February) in Rennes is mild but can be damp and chilly, with temperatures averaging around 3°C to 8°C (37°F to 46°F). While snowfall is rare, the city's historic streets and monuments take on a magical atmosphere during the holiday season, with festive decorations and seasonal markets adding to the festive spirit.

Spring (March - May) heralds the return of warmer weather and blooming flowers, as Rennes awakens from its winter slumber. It is an ideal time to explore the city's parks and botanical gardens, embark on scenic bike rides along the river trails, or take day trips to nearby attractions such as the Mont Saint-Michel or the Emerald Coast.

Overall, Rennes' mild climate and scenic surroundings make it a delightful destination to visit year-round, offering something for every traveler to enjoy, whether they're seeking outdoor adventure, cultural immersion, or simply a peaceful retreat in nature.

Culture and Language

Rennes boasts a rich cultural heritage shaped by its Celtic roots, Breton traditions, and dynamic urban culture. From its ancient monuments and historic landmarks to its vibrant arts scene and culinary delights, Rennes offers visitors a captivating glimpse into its diverse cultural landscape.

Breton Influence:

Breton culture plays a significant role in shaping the identity of Rennes and the wider Brittany region. The Bretons are descendants of Celtic tribes who migrated to the area during the early Middle Ages, bringing with them their language, traditions, and folklore. While French is the dominant language spoken in Rennes, Breton is still spoken and celebrated by a passionate minority, particularly in rural communities and cultural festivals.

Breton music, dance, and storytelling are integral parts of the cultural fabric of Rennes, with traditional festivals such as the Fest Noz (night festival) showcasing lively performances of folk music and dance. Visitors to Rennes can immerse themselves in Breton culture by attending cultural events, visiting museums dedicated to Breton heritage, or sampling regional delicacies made with locally sourced ingredients.

Arts and Literature:

Rennes has long been a center of artistic and literary creativity, attracting artists, writers, and intellectuals from across France and beyond. The city's historic streets and landmarks have inspired generations of painters, poets, and playwrights, with notable figures such as the surrealist artist Jean Cocteau and the poet Paul Éluard finding inspiration in its picturesque surroundings.

Today, Rennes continues to foster a vibrant arts scene, with numerous galleries, theaters, and cultural institutions showcasing the work of local and international artists. The Frac Bretagne, Rennes' contemporary art center, hosts rotating exhibitions of modern and contemporary art, while the Théâtre National de Bretagne (National Theater of Brittany) presents a diverse program of theater, dance, and performance art.

Language and Linguistic Diversity:

While French is the primary language spoken in Rennes, the city's linguistic landscape is characterized by a rich diversity of languages and dialects. In addition to Breton, which is spoken by a minority of residents, Rennes is home to a growing community of international students, expatriates, and immigrants, who bring with them a multitude of languages and cultures.

The presence of universities and research institutes in Rennes contributes to its linguistic diversity, with students and scholars from around the world converging in the city to study, conduct research, and exchange ideas. Visitors to Rennes may encounter a variety of languages spoken on the streets, in cafes, and in cultural events, reflecting the city's cosmopolitan character and global outlook.

In conclusion, Rennes' cultural richness and linguistic diversity make it a fascinating destination for travelers seeking to immerse themselves in the heritage and traditions of Brittany. Whether exploring the city's historic landmarks, attending cultural events, or sampling its culinary delights, visitors to Rennes are sure to be enchanted by its vibrant cultural tapestry and warm hospitality.

Local Cuisine and Culinary Delights

Rennes is renowned for its rich culinary heritage, which reflects the region's maritime bounty, agricultural abundance, and Celtic traditions. From savory crepes and hearty stews to fresh seafood and artisanal cheeses, Rennes offers visitors a delectable array of culinary delights to tantalize the taste buds.

Breton Gastronomy:

Breton cuisine is characterized by its use of fresh, locally sourced ingredients, simple yet flavorful dishes, and a strong emphasis on seafood and dairy products. Rennes, as a major city in Brittany, proudly showcases the best of Breton gastronomy, with its markets, restaurants, and cafes offering a diverse selection of traditional dishes and regional specialties.

Crepes and Galettes:

One of the most iconic dishes of Breton cuisine is the crepe, a thin pancake made from buckwheat flour and typically filled with sweet or savory ingredients. In Rennes, visitors can indulge in a variety of crepes, from the classic "complète" with ham, cheese, and egg to more creative combinations featuring local cheeses, seafood, and vegetables.

Galettes, a savory variation of the crepe made with buckwheat flour, are also popular in Rennes. Traditionally served with savory fillings such as ham, cheese, and mushrooms, galettes are a hearty and satisfying meal that can be enjoyed any time of day.

Seafood Specialties:

Located just a short distance from the coast, Rennes enjoys access to some of the freshest seafood in France, which is reflected in its culinary offerings. Visitors to Rennes can sample an array of seafood specialties, including oysters from nearby Cancale, mussels from the Bay of Mont Saint-Michel, and fresh fish such as sole, sea bass, and cod.

One popular seafood dish in Rennes is "moules marinières," or mussels cooked in a white wine and garlic broth, served with crusty bread for dipping. Another local favorite is "galette-saucisse," a grilled sausage wrapped in a savory crepe and typically enjoyed at outdoor festivals and street markets.

Artisanal Cheeses and Dairy Products:

Brittany is known for its rich dairy heritage, with an abundance of cows, goats, and sheep grazing on the region's lush pastures. As a result, Rennes boasts a wide variety of artisanal cheeses and dairy products, including creamy Camembert, tangy Roquefort, and pungent Pont l'Évêque.

Visitors to Rennes can sample these cheeses at local markets, cheese shops, and restaurants, where they are often served alongside crusty bread, local honey, and preserves. Dairy products such as butter, cream, and yogurt are also key ingredients in many Breton dishes, adding richness and flavor to traditional recipes.

In conclusion, Rennes' culinary scene is a reflection of the region's rich cultural heritage, with its emphasis on fresh, locally sourced ingredients, traditional cooking techniques, and bold flavors. Whether indulging in savory crepes, savoring fresh seafood, or sampling artisanal cheeses, visitors to Rennes are sure to delight in the city's culinary delights and gastronomic treasures.

Chapter Two: Exploring Rennes City Center

Historic Landmarks and Monuments

Rennes is steeped in history and boasts a wealth of historic landmarks and monuments that showcase its rich cultural heritage. From medieval cathedrals and ancient city walls to grand palaces and charming squares, Rennes offers visitors a fascinating journey through time.

Rennes Cathedral (Cathédrale Saint-Pierre de Rennes):

One of the most iconic landmarks in Rennes is its majestic cathedral, dedicated to Saint Peter. Built between the 11th and 18th centuries, the Rennes Cathedral is a masterpiece of Gothic architecture, with its soaring spires, intricate stone carvings, and stunning stained glass windows.

Visitors to the cathedral can admire its impressive facade, adorned with statues of saints and biblical figures, before stepping inside to explore its richly decorated interior. Highlights include the beautiful rose window, the ornate choir stalls, and the tomb of Jean-Baptiste de la Salle, the founder of the Institute of the Brothers of the Christian Schools.

Parlement de Bretagne:

Another iconic landmark in Rennes is the Parlement de Bretagne, or Parliament of Brittany, a historic courthouse located in the heart of the city. Built in the 17th century in the classical French style, the Parlement de Bretagne is renowned for its imposing facade, adorned with Corinthian columns, statues, and bas-reliefs depicting scenes from Breton history.

While the Parlement de Bretagne no longer serves as a judicial institution, it remains an important symbol of Brittany's cultural and political heritage. Visitors can admire its grandeur from the outside or take guided tours of its interior, which includes a magnificent courtroom and an impressive library.

City Walls and Gates:

Rennes' medieval city walls and gates are another testament to its rich architectural heritage. Originally constructed in the 3rd century by the Romans, the city walls were later expanded and reinforced during the Middle Ages to protect the city from invaders.

Today, several sections of the city walls and gates still stand, offering visitors a glimpse into Rennes' medieval past. The Portes Mordelaises, a fortified gatehouse dating back to the 15th century, is one of the most well-preserved sections of the city walls and now houses a museum dedicated to the history of Rennes.

Place des Lices:

The Place des Lices is a historic square in the heart of Rennes, famous for its bustling market and lively atmosphere. Dating back to the Middle Ages, the square was once used for jousting tournaments and other festive events.

Today, the Place des Lices is home to one of the largest markets in Brittany, where vendors sell everything from fresh produce and local specialties to clothing, crafts, and antiques. Visitors can wander through the market stalls, sample regional delicacies, and soak up the vibrant ambiance of this historic square.

In conclusion, Rennes' historic landmarks and monuments offer visitors a fascinating glimpse into the city's rich cultural heritage and architectural legacy. Whether exploring its medieval cathedrals, ancient city walls, or bustling squares, visitors to Rennes are sure to be enchanted by its timeless beauty and storied past.

Vibrant Markets and Shopping Districts

Rennes is renowned for its vibrant markets and bustling shopping districts, where visitors can immerse themselves in the local culture, sample regional delicacies, and shop for unique souvenirs and gifts. From historic marketplaces to modern shopping centers, Rennes offers a diverse array of shopping experiences to suit every taste and budget.

Marché des Lices:

One of the must-visit attractions in Rennes is the Marché des Lices, one of the largest and oldest markets in France. Held every Saturday morning in the historic center of Rennes, the Marché des Lices is a feast for the senses, with over 290 stalls selling a wide variety of products, including fresh produce, seafood, meats, cheeses, bread, pastries, flowers, and artisanal crafts.

Visitors to the Marché des Lices can wander through the bustling aisles, sampling local specialties such as crepes, oysters, and cider, while soaking up the vibrant atmosphere of this iconic market. The market also hosts occasional events, such as cooking demonstrations, live music performances, and cultural exhibitions, adding to the excitement and charm of the experience.

Sainte-Anne Market:

Located in the lively Sainte-Anne district, the Sainte-Anne Market is another popular destination for food lovers and bargain hunters in Rennes. Open daily, this covered market features a diverse selection of vendors selling fresh produce, meats, cheeses, seafood, spices, and gourmet specialties from Brittany and beyond.

In addition to its food stalls, the Sainte-Anne Market also offers a variety of non-food items, including clothing, accessories, household goods, and handicrafts. Visitors can explore the market's narrow alleys and hidden corners, discovering hidden gems and unique finds while enjoying the bustling ambiance of this local favorite.

Shopping Districts:

In addition to its vibrant markets, Rennes is home to several shopping districts and commercial areas, where visitors can find a wide range of shops, boutiques, department stores, and specialty stores offering everything from fashion and accessories to electronics, home goods, and souvenirs.

The Rue Saint-Michel is one of the main shopping streets in Rennes, lined with trendy boutiques, designer shops, and international brands. Visitors can browse the latest fashion trends, shop for stylish accessories, or sample gourmet treats at artisanal food shops and bakeries along this bustling thoroughfare.

For those seeking a more modern shopping experience, Rennes boasts several shopping centers and malls, including the Centre Commercial Alma and the Centre

Commercial Colombia. These shopping centers feature a mix of national and international retailers, as well as restaurants, cafes, and entertainment options, making them ideal destinations for a day of shopping and leisure.

In conclusion, Rennes' vibrant markets and shopping districts offer visitors a diverse and dynamic shopping experience, where they can discover the best of Brittany's culinary delights, artisanal crafts, and fashion trends while immersing themselves in the local culture and ambiance. Whether exploring the historic Marché des Lices, browsing the trendy boutiques of Rue Saint-Michel, or indulging in retail therapy at a modern shopping center, visitors to Rennes are sure to find something to delight and inspire them.

Cultural Institutions and Museums

Rennes is home to a rich cultural heritage and boasts a variety of museums, galleries, and cultural institutions that showcase the region's history, art, and traditions. From ancient artifacts and contemporary art to interactive exhibits and immersive experiences, Rennes offers visitors a diverse array of cultural attractions to explore and enjoy.

Musée des Beaux-Arts:

The Musée des Beaux-Arts de Rennes, or Museum of Fine Arts, is one of the oldest and most prestigious art museums in France, housing an impressive collection of paintings, sculptures, and decorative arts spanning from the Middle Ages to the present day. Housed in a historic 19th-century building near the city center, the museum's permanent collection includes works by renowned artists such as Rubens, Delacroix, Monet, Picasso, and Rodin.

In addition to its permanent collection, the Musée des Beaux-Arts also hosts temporary exhibitions, educational programs, and cultural events throughout the year, making it a must-visit destination for art lovers and enthusiasts of all ages.

Les Champs Libres:

Les Champs Libres is a cultural complex located in the heart of Rennes, housing three major institutions under one roof: the Musée de Bretagne (Museum of Brittany), the Espace des Sciences (Space of

Sciences), and the Bibliothèque de Rennes Métropole (Rennes Metropolitan Library). This innovative cultural hub offers visitors a wide range of experiences, from exploring the history and heritage of Brittany to discovering the latest advances in science and technology.

The Musée de Bretagne showcases the history, culture, and traditions of Brittany through a variety of interactive exhibits, artifacts, and multimedia installations. Visitors can learn about the region's Celtic roots, maritime heritage, and contemporary identity, while exploring topics such as agriculture, industry, and folklore.

The Espace des Sciences offers visitors a journey through the wonders of the universe, with hands-on exhibits, multimedia presentations, and interactive workshops exploring topics such as astronomy, physics, and biology. Visitors can explore the mysteries of the cosmos, conduct experiments, and engage with cutting-edge research in a fun and educational environment.

The Bibliothèque de Rennes Métropole is a modern library and cultural center, offering a vast collection of books, multimedia resources, and cultural events for visitors of all ages. From literary readings and film screenings to workshops and conferences, the library provides a vibrant space for learning, discovery, and creativity.

Other Cultural Institutions and Museums:

In addition to the Musée des Beaux-Arts and Les Champs Libres, Rennes is home to several other cultural institutions and museums worth exploring. The Musée de la Danse (Dance Museum) celebrates the art of dance through exhibitions, performances, and educational programs, while the Centre d'Histoire de Rennes et de Bretagne (Center for the History of Rennes and Brittany) offers insights into the city's past through archival documents, photographs, and artifacts.

Other notable museums in Rennes include the Musée de la Faïence (Museum of Faience), dedicated to the history and craftsmanship of ceramics in Brittany, and the Ecomusée du Pays de Rennes (Ecomuseum of the Rennes Region), which explores the rural heritage and traditions of the surrounding countryside.

In conclusion, Rennes' cultural institutions and museums offer visitors a fascinating journey through the region's history, art, and culture, providing opportunities for learning, discovery, and inspiration. Whether exploring the masterpieces of the Musée des Beaux-Arts, delving into the history of Brittany at Les Champs Libres, or discovering the rich heritage of Rennes and its surroundings, visitors to Rennes are sure to find something to ignite their curiosity and enrich their experience of the city.

Chapter Three: Discovering the Surrounding Areas

Day Trips from Rennes

While Rennes offers a wealth of attractions and experiences, its strategic location in the heart of Brittany also makes it an ideal base for exploring the region's diverse landscapes, historic sites, and cultural treasures. From ancient castles and charming coastal villages to scenic countryside and natural parks, Rennes serves as the perfect starting point for a variety of memorable day trips.

Mont Saint-Michel:

One of the most iconic and popular day trips from Rennes is a visit to Mont Saint-Michel, a UNESCO World Heritage site located just 60 kilometers northwest of the city. Perched on a rocky island in the midst of vast tidal flats, Mont Saint-Michel is renowned for its stunning medieval architecture, narrow cobblestone streets, and panoramic views of the surrounding coastline.

Visitors can explore the abbey, which dates back to the 8th century and houses a remarkable collection of religious artifacts and works of art, or wander through the charming village below, with its quaint shops, cafes, and museums. Guided tours, boat rides, and scenic walks along the coastal path provide opportunities to immerse oneself in the history and natural beauty of this iconic landmark.

Saint-Malo:

Another popular day trip destination from Rennes is the historic port city of Saint-Malo, located approximately 70 kilometers northwest along the rugged coastline of Brittany. Famous for its well-preserved medieval ramparts, picturesque harbor, and maritime heritage, Saint-Malo offers visitors a glimpse into the region's seafaring past and vibrant present.

Visitors can stroll along the city walls, explore the narrow alleys of the old town, and visit attractions such as the Château de Saint-Malo, the Musée d'Histoire de la Ville et du Pays Malouin (Museum of the History of Saint-Malo), and the Fort National, a 17th-century fortress perched on a rocky island just offshore. The city's sandy beaches, lively markets, and seafood restaurants also make it a popular destination for day-trippers seeking sun, surf, and culinary delights.

Dinan:

Nestled along the banks of the Rance River, just 50 kilometers northwest of Rennes, is the charming medieval town of Dinan. With its well-preserved timber-framed buildings, cobblestone streets, and imposing ramparts, Dinan is a delightful destination for history buffs and architecture enthusiasts alike.

Visitors to Dinan can explore the town's medieval fortifications, including the 13th-century Château de Dinan and the Tour de l'Horloge, a clock tower that offers panoramic views of the surrounding countryside. Other highlights include the Basilique Saint-Sauveur, a Romanesque church dating back to the 12th century, and the Musée du Château de Dinan, which houses exhibits on the town's history and heritage.

Brocéliande Forest:

For nature lovers and outdoor enthusiasts, a day trip to the Brocéliande Forest offers a tranquil escape into Brittany's enchanting woodlands and mythical landscapes. Located approximately 70 kilometers southwest of Rennes, the Brocéliande Forest is steeped in legend and folklore, with tales of King Arthur, Merlin the wizard, and the Lady of the Lake weaving through its ancient groves.

Visitors can explore the forest's scenic trails, discover hidden waterfalls and picturesque ponds, and visit landmarks such as the Val sans Retour (Valley of No Return), the Tomb of Merlin, and the Fountain of Barenton. Guided tours, storytelling sessions, and themed events provide opportunities to delve deeper into the mysteries and magic of this legendary forest.

In conclusion, Rennes' strategic location and excellent transportation links make it an ideal base for exploring the diverse attractions and landscapes of Brittany. Whether venturing to the historic island of Mont Saint-Michel, the fortified city of Saint-Malo, the medieval town of Dinan, or the enchanted Brocéliande Forest, day-trippers from Rennes are sure to find adventure, beauty, and inspiration at every turn.

Outdoor Adventures and Nature Reserves

Rennes, the capital city of Brittany in northwestern France, is surrounded by breathtaking natural landscapes, from lush forests and scenic rivers to rugged coastlines and tranquil countryside. Outdoor enthusiasts and nature lovers will find no shortage of opportunities for adventure and exploration in the region, with a variety of nature reserves, parks, and outdoor activities to enjoy.

Brocéliande Forest:

One of the most enchanting outdoor destinations near Rennes is the Brocéliande Forest, a mythical woodland steeped in legend and folklore. Covering over 7,000 hectares of ancient oaks, beech trees, and heathlands, the Brocéliande Forest offers visitors a tranquil escape into Brittany's magical landscapes.

Hikers and nature lovers can explore the forest's scenic trails, which wind through moss-covered glades, hidden waterfalls, and mystical groves. Highlights include the Val sans Retour (Valley of No Return), the Tomb of Merlin, and the Fountain of Barenton, all of which are associated with the tales of King Arthur and the Knights of the Round Table.

Armorique Regional Natural Park:

Located just a short drive from Rennes, the Armorique Regional Natural Park encompasses over 125,000 hectares of pristine coastline, rugged cliffs, and picturesque countryside. Stretching from the Crozon Peninsula to the Monts d'Arrée, the park offers visitors a diverse array of landscapes and outdoor activities to enjoy.

Hikers can explore the park's network of trails, which wind through ancient forests, heathlands, and coastal dunes, offering panoramic views of the Atlantic Ocean and the surrounding countryside. Birdwatchers can spot a variety of avian species, including seabirds, waders, and migratory birds, while nature enthusiasts can discover hidden waterfalls, meandering rivers, and secluded beaches along the park's coastline.

Ille-et-Rance Canal:

For those seeking a more leisurely outdoor experience, the Ille-et-Rance Canal offers a scenic setting for boating, kayaking, and cycling along its tranquil waters. Stretching over 85 kilometers from Rennes to Saint-Malo, the canal winds through picturesque countryside, charming villages, and historic landmarks, providing opportunities for relaxation and exploration along the way.

Visitors can rent kayaks or canoes to paddle along the canal, stopping at riverside cafes and picnic spots to refuel and enjoy the scenery. Cyclists can follow the towpaths that run parallel to the canal, passing through scenic countryside and charming villages, with plenty of opportunities to stop and explore local attractions along the way.

Marais de la Briantais:

Located just south of Rennes, the Marais de la Briantais is a peaceful nature reserve that offers visitors a tranquil retreat from the hustle and bustle of city life. Covering over 100 hectares of marshes, wetlands, and meadows, the reserve is home to a variety of wildlife, including birds, amphibians, and rare plant species.

Visitors can explore the reserve's network of walking trails and boardwalks, which wind through diverse habitats and offer opportunities for birdwatching, photography, and nature observation. Interpretive signs and guided tours provide insights into the ecology and biodiversity of the reserve, making it a rewarding destination for nature enthusiasts of all ages.

In conclusion, Rennes and its surrounding region offer a wealth of outdoor adventures and nature reserves for visitors to explore and enjoy. Whether hiking through the enchanted forests of Brocéliande, kayaking along the tranquil waters of the Ille-et-Rance Canal, or birdwatching in the marshes of Marais de la Briantais, outdoor enthusiasts will find endless opportunities for adventure and discovery in this beautiful corner of Brittany.

Charming Villages and Towns Nearby

Beyond the bustling streets of Rennes lie a plethora of charming villages and towns that offer visitors a glimpse into the rich history, culture, and traditions of Brittany. From medieval fortresses and half-timbered houses to coastal fishing villages and picturesque countryside, these idyllic destinations provide the perfect escape from the hustle and bustle of city life.

Dinan:

Located just a short drive from Rennes, the medieval town of Dinan is a picturesque gem nestled along the banks of the Rance River. With its well-preserved timber-framed buildings, cobblestone streets, and imposing ramparts, Dinan exudes old-world charm and medieval splendor.

Visitors to Dinan can wander through the town's narrow alleys and hidden courtyards, discovering quaint shops, cafes, and galleries tucked away in centuries-old buildings. Highlights include the Château de Dinan, a 13th-century fortress overlooking the river, and the Basilique Saint-Sauveur, a

Romanesque church adorned with intricate carvings and stained glass windows.

Saint-Suliac:

Perched on the banks of the Rance River, just a short drive from Rennes, is the charming fishing village of Saint-Suliac. Known for its picturesque harbor, colorful fishing boats, and winding streets lined with traditional stone houses, Saint-Suliac offers visitors a tranquil retreat in a stunning coastal setting.

Visitors to Saint-Suliac can stroll along the waterfront promenade, admiring views of the river and surrounding countryside, or explore the village's narrow alleys and hidden courtyards, discovering quaint shops, art galleries, and cafes along the way. The village also hosts several festivals and events throughout the year, celebrating its maritime heritage and cultural traditions.

Combourg:

Located approximately 40 kilometers northwest of Rennes, the town of Combourg is a charming medieval enclave steeped in history and romance. Dominated by the imposing silhouette of the Château de Combourg, a medieval fortress perched atop a rocky promontory, Combourg exudes a sense of timeless elegance and grandeur.

Visitors to Combourg can explore the cobblestone streets of the old town, admiring the half-timbered houses, ancient churches, and historic landmarks that dot the landscape. Highlights include the Château de Combourg, once home to the renowned writer Chateaubriand, and the

Église Sainte-Marie, a Gothic church dating back to the 15th century.

Cancale:

Located along the rugged coastline of Brittany, just a short drive from Rennes, is the charming fishing village of Cancale. Famous for its oysters, fresh seafood, and stunning coastal scenery, Cancale offers visitors a taste of traditional Breton culture and maritime heritage.

Visitors to Cancale can stroll along the picturesque harbor, watching the fishing boats come and go, or explore the village's narrow streets and charming squares, lined with seafood restaurants, creperies, and artisanal shops. The nearby Pointe du Grouin offers panoramic views of the coastline and is a popular spot for hiking, picnicking, and birdwatching.

In conclusion, the charming villages and towns near Rennes offer visitors a delightful escape into the heart of Brittany, with their medieval architecture, coastal charm, and picturesque countryside providing the perfect backdrop for exploring the region's rich history, culture, and natural beauty. Whether wandering through the cobblestone streets of Dinan, admiring the coastal vistas of Saint-Suliac, exploring the historic landmarks of Combourg, or sampling fresh oysters in Cancale, visitors to these idyllic destinations are sure to be enchanted by their timeless allure and warm hospitality.

Chapter Four: Experiencing Rennes Nightlife and Entertainment

Bars, Pubs, and Nightclubs

Rennes comes alive at night with a diverse array of bars, pubs, and nightclubs that cater to all tastes and preferences. Whether you're looking for a cozy pub to enjoy a pint of local beer, a trendy cocktail bar to sip on craft cocktails, or a lively nightclub to dance the night away, Rennes has something for everyone.

Bars and Pubs:

Rue Saint-Michel: This bustling street in the heart of Rennes is home to a variety of bars and pubs, offering everything from traditional Irish pubs and cozy wine bars to hip craft beer joints and trendy cocktail lounges. Visitors can hop from one establishment to the next, sampling local brews, artisanal cocktails, and regional wines while soaking up the lively atmosphere of this popular nightlife district.

Le Saint-Patrick: Located in the historic center of Rennes, Le Saint-Patrick is a charming Irish pub known for its cozy atmosphere, friendly staff, and impressive selection of beers and whiskies. Visitors can relax in the pub's traditional interior, complete with wooden furnishings, exposed brick walls, and live music performances, while enjoying a pint of Guinness or sampling one of the pub's specialty cocktails.

La Bascule: Tucked away in a historic building near the Place des Lices, La Bascule is a popular hangout spot for locals and visitors alike. This cozy bar features a laid-back ambiance, eclectic decor, and a rotating selection of craft beers, ciders, and cocktails. Visitors can unwind on the outdoor terrace, mingle with fellow patrons, and enjoy live music and DJ sets on select nights.

Nightclubs:

Le Liberté: Situated in a former theater building in the city center, Le Liberté is one of the largest and most popular nightclubs in Rennes. This multi-level venue features multiple dance floors, VIP lounges, and state-of-the-art sound and lighting systems, making it a favorite destination for partygoers and music lovers. Le Liberté hosts a variety of themed nights, live performances, and guest DJs, ensuring a lively and unforgettable nightlife experience.

Ubu: Located near the train station, Ubu is a legendary nightclub and live music venue that has been a staple of Rennes' nightlife scene for decades. This iconic venue hosts a diverse lineup of concerts, DJ sets, and club nights, featuring everything from indie rock and electronic music to hip-hop and reggae. With its spacious dance floor, intimate atmosphere, and cutting-edge sound system, Ubu offers an unparalleled nightlife experience for music enthusiasts of all genres.

Le 1988: Situated in the trendy Saint-Anne district, Le 1988 is a stylish nightclub and cocktail bar known for its sleek decor, upscale ambiance, and top-notch mixology. This exclusive venue features a chic lounge area, VIP booths, and a rooftop terrace with panoramic views of the city skyline. Visitors can sip on expertly crafted cocktails, dance to the beats of resident DJs, and mingle with Rennes' stylish crowd late into the night.

In conclusion, Rennes' bars, pubs, and nightclubs offer visitors a diverse and dynamic nightlife experience, with something for every taste and mood. Whether you're sipping on local brews in a cozy pub, dancing the night away in a trendy nightclub, or enjoying craft cocktails in a stylish lounge, Rennes' vibrant nightlife scene is sure to leave you with unforgettable memories and a desire to come back for more.

Live Music and Performance Venues

Rennes, the cultural hub of Brittany in northwestern France, boasts a thriving live music scene with a variety of venues that cater to music lovers of all genres. From intimate concert halls and historic theaters to cozy cafes and outdoor amphitheaters, Rennes offers a diverse array of options for experiencing live music and performances.

Le Liberté:

Le Liberté is one of Rennes' premier live music venues, housed in a historic theater building in the city center. With a capacity of over 5,000 people, Le Liberté hosts a wide range of concerts, performances, and events throughout the year, featuring both national and international artists across a variety of genres, including rock, pop, jazz, classical, and world music. The venue's state-of-the-art sound and lighting systems, along with its spacious dance floor and comfortable seating options, ensure an unforgettable live music experience for audiences of all ages.

Ubu:

Ubu is a legendary live music venue and nightclub located near the train station in Rennes. This iconic venue has been a staple of the city's music scene for decades, hosting a diverse lineup of concerts, DJ sets, and club nights featuring both emerging and established artists from around the world.

With its intimate atmosphere, cutting-edge sound system, and eclectic programming, Ubu offers a unique and immersive live music experience that appeals to music enthusiasts of all tastes and backgrounds.

L'Étage:

L'Étage is a popular live music venue and performance space located in the heart of Rennes' historic center. This intimate venue features a cozy atmosphere, with a small stage and seating area that provides an up-close and personal experience for both artists and audiences. L'Étage hosts a variety of concerts, open mic nights, and jam sessions showcasing local talent and emerging artists from across France and beyond, making it a favorite destination for music lovers looking to discover new sounds and support up-and-coming musicians.

Le Mondo Bizarro:

Le Mondo Bizarro is a unique live music venue and cultural center located in the eclectic Saint-Anne district of Rennes. This intimate space features a laid-back ambiance, with quirky decor, colorful murals, and comfortable seating areas that create a welcoming atmosphere for artists and audiences alike. Le Mondo Bizarro hosts a diverse range of performances, including concerts, poetry readings, theater productions, and art exhibitions, with a focus on promoting creativity, diversity, and community engagement. Visitors can enjoy live music in a relaxed and inclusive environment, surrounded by like-minded individuals who share a passion for art, culture, and self-expression.

La Citrouille:

La Citrouille is a dynamic live music venue and cultural center located on the outskirts of Rennes. Housed in a former squash court, this unique space features a flexible layout, with a main stage area that can accommodate both intimate acoustic performances and high-energy concerts. La Citrouille hosts a wide range of events, including concerts, festivals, workshops, and community gatherings, with a focus on promoting local talent and fostering creative expression. Visitors can experience live music in a vibrant and inclusive atmosphere, surrounded by artists, musicians, and enthusiasts who share a love for music and culture.

In conclusion, Rennes' live music and performance venues offer visitors a diverse and dynamic array of options for experiencing the city's vibrant cultural scene. Whether you're into rock, jazz, classical, or world music, there's something for everyone to enjoy in Rennes' thriving live music scene. So grab your tickets, head out to a venue, and immerse yourself in the electrifying energy of live music in Brittany's capital city.

Festivals and Events Calendar

Rennes offers a year-round calendar of festivals and events that attract visitors from near and far.

Festival des Tombées de la Nuit:

Date: July-August

The Festival des Tombées de la Nuit is one of Rennes' most anticipated summer events, featuring a diverse lineup of outdoor performances, concerts, theater productions, and street art installations. Held over several weeks in July and August, the festival transforms the city into a colorful and vibrant playground for artists and audiences alike, with events taking place in parks, squares, and historic landmarks throughout Rennes.

Les Trans Musicales:

Date: December

Les Trans Musicales is an internationally renowned music festival that takes place annually in December, showcasing emerging artists and cutting-edge musical trends from around the world. Founded in 1979, the festival has earned a reputation for its eclectic programming, innovative spirit, and electric atmosphere, with performances spanning a wide range of genres, including rock, electronic, hip-hop, and world music. With multiple venues across the city hosting concerts, DJ sets, and special events, Les Trans Musicales offers music lovers a unique opportunity to discover new sounds and experience the excitement of live music in Rennes.

Fête de la Musique:

Date: June

The Fête de la Musique, also known as World Music Day, is celebrated annually on June 21st in cities and towns across France, including Rennes. This nationwide event showcases the diversity and vitality of the country's music scene, with free concerts and performances taking place in public spaces, parks, and venues throughout the city. From rock and pop to jazz and classical, the Fête de la Musique offers something for everyone to enjoy, with musicians of all ages and backgrounds sharing their talents and spreading the joy of music to audiences of all ages.

Festival Yaouank:

Date: November

Festival Yaouank is Brittany's largest traditional music and dance festival, celebrating the region's rich Celtic heritage and cultural traditions. Held annually in November, the festival features a diverse lineup of concerts, workshops, and dance performances, showcasing the best of

Breton music, song, and dance. Visitors can experience the thrill of traditional Breton fest-noz dances, sample regional delicacies, and immerse themselves in the vibrant atmosphere of this beloved cultural event.

Marché à Manger:

Date: Monthly (Summer)

Marché à Manger is a monthly food festival held in Rennes during the summer months, celebrating the region's culinary delights and gastronomic traditions. Taking place in parks, squares, and outdoor venues across the city, the festival features a wide variety of food stalls, pop-up restaurants, and gourmet food trucks offering everything from local specialties and international cuisine to artisanal products and street food favorites. Visitors can sample a diverse array of flavors, dine al fresco with friends and family, and enjoy live music, entertainment, and cultural activities throughout the day and into the evening.

Rennes sur Roulettes:

Date: May

Rennes sur Roulettes is an annual roller skating festival held in May, attracting enthusiasts from across France and beyond to participate in a weekend of roller skating, skateboarding, and other wheeled sports. The festival features a variety of events and competitions for skaters of all ages and skill levels, including street races, freestyle performances, and skatepark challenges. Visitors can watch thrilling demonstrations, try out new equipment, and join in the fun with activities and workshops for beginners and experienced skaters alike.

Travelling Film Festival:

Date: February-March

The Travelling Film Festival is an annual event that celebrates the art of cinema and showcases a diverse selection of films from around the world. Held in February and March, the festival features screenings, premieres, and retrospectives at theaters, cinemas, and cultural venues throughout Rennes. From independent documentaries and arthouse classics to blockbuster hits and international favorites, the Travelling Film Festival offers something for cinephiles of all tastes and interests, with opportunities to meet filmmakers, attend Q&A sessions, and participate in discussions and workshops.

In conclusion, Rennes' festivals and events calendar offers a diverse and dynamic lineup of cultural experiences that showcase the region's creativity, diversity, and community spirit. Whether you're into music, dance, food, film, or sports, there's something for everyone to enjoy in Rennes' vibrant cultural scene. So mark your calendars, book your tickets, and get ready to immerse yourself in the excitement and energy of these unforgettable events in Brittany's capital city.

Chapter Five: Practical Information and Travel Tips

Accommodation Options and Recommendations

Rennes, the capital city of Brittany in northwestern France, offers visitors a wide range of accommodation options to suit every budget, preference, and travel style. From luxury hotels and boutique guesthouses to budget-friendly hostels and cozy bed and breakfasts, Rennes has something for everyone. Here are some recommendations for accommodation options in the city:

Luxury Hotels:

1. Balthazar Hotel & Spa:
Located in the heart of Rennes' historic center, Balthazar Hotel & Spa offers luxurious accommodations with elegant decor, modern amenities, and personalized service. The hotel features spacious rooms and suites with comfortable beds, stylish furnishings, and marble bathrooms, as well as a rooftop terrace, spa, and gourmet restaurant.

2. Le Saint-Antoine Hotel & Spa:
Situated in a historic building near the Parliament of Brittany, Le Saint-Antoine Hotel & Spa combines old-world charm with modern sophistication. The hotel features

beautifully appointed rooms and suites with period details, plush bedding, and contemporary amenities, as well as a spa, fitness center, and fine dining restaurant.

Boutique Hotels:

1. Hotel Anne de Bretagne:
Nestled in the Sainte-Anne district, Hotel Anne de Bretagne is a charming boutique hotel with stylish rooms and personalized service. The hotel features cozy accommodations with colorful decor, comfortable beds, and modern amenities, as well as a garden terrace, lounge area, and breakfast buffet.

2. Lecoq-Gadby Hotel & Spa:
Located in a 19th-century mansion surrounded by lush gardens, Lecoq-Gadby Hotel & Spa offers a tranquil retreat in the

heart of Rennes. The hotel features elegantly appointed rooms and suites with antique furnishings, luxurious bedding, and spa-like bathrooms, as well as a wellness center, outdoor pool, and gourmet restaurant.

Budget-Friendly Options:

1. Le Magic Hall:
Le Magic Hall is a quirky and budget-friendly hotel located in the historic center of Rennes. The hotel features themed rooms with unique decor, comfortable beds, and basic amenities, as well as a cozy lounge area, library, and communal kitchenette.

2. ibis Budget Rennes Centre Gare:
Conveniently located near the train station, ibis Budget Rennes Centre Gare offers affordable accommodations with modern

comforts and amenities. The hotel features simple yet comfortable rooms with cozy bedding, en-suite bathrooms, and complimentary Wi-Fi, as well as a continental breakfast buffet and 24-hour reception.

Alternative Accommodation:

1. Airbnb:

For those seeking a more personalized and unique lodging experience, Airbnb offers a variety of apartments, studios, and private rooms for rent in Rennes. Visitors can choose from a range of accommodations, from cozy lofts and historic townhouses to modern apartments and countryside retreats, with options to suit every budget and preference.

2. Hostels:

Rennes also offers several budget-friendly hostels for backpackers, solo travelers, and budget-conscious visitors. Hostels such as Le Flâneur Guesthouse and Ho36 Hostel & Bar provide affordable dormitory-style accommodations with shared facilities, as well as communal spaces, social activities, and a welcoming atmosphere for guests to enjoy.

In conclusion, Rennes offers a variety of accommodation options to suit every traveler's needs and preferences, from luxury hotels and boutique guesthouses to budget-friendly hostels and alternative lodging options. Whether you're seeking a luxurious retreat, a cozy home away from home, or a budget-friendly base for exploring the city, Rennes has something for everyone to enjoy.

Transportation Guide: Getting Around Rennes

Rennes boasts an efficient and accessible transportation network that makes getting around the city and its surrounding areas easy and convenient. From public transit and bicycles to taxis and rental cars, Rennes offers a variety of transportation options to suit every traveler's needs and preferences. Here is a detailed guide to getting around Rennes:

Public Transit:

Rennes Métropole Transit System (STAR):

The Rennes Métropole transit system, known as STAR, operates an extensive network of buses and metro lines that serve the city and its suburbs. The buses and metro run regularly throughout the day and into the evening, providing reliable and affordable transportation for residents and visitors alike. Tickets can be purchased at ticket vending machines located at metro stations, bus stops, and select retailers, with options for single rides, day passes, and multi-day passes available.

The Metro:

The Rennes metro system consists of a single line, Line A, which runs from north to south through the city center, with stops at key destinations such as the train station, the Parliament of Brittany, and the university campus. The metro operates every 3 to 5 minutes during peak hours and every 7 to 10 minutes during off-peak hours, making it a convenient option for getting around quickly and efficiently.

Bus Services:

In addition to the metro, the STAR transit system operates over 50 bus routes that connect neighborhoods, suburbs, and outlying areas of Rennes. The buses run regularly throughout the day and evening, with service extending into the late night on select routes. Bus stops are clearly marked with route numbers and schedules, and electronic displays provide real-time information on arrival times and service disruptions.

Bicycles:

VéloStar Bike-Sharing Program:

Rennes offers a bike-sharing program called VéloStar, which allows residents and visitors to rent bicycles for short trips around the city. Bicycles can be rented from stations located throughout Rennes and returned to any station within the network. Users can sign up for a subscription online or at a station kiosk, with options for daily, weekly, or monthly passes available. The VéloStar program offers a convenient and eco-friendly way to explore Rennes at your own pace.

Taxis:

Taxis Rennais:

Taxis Rennais is the main taxi company serving Rennes and its surrounding areas, offering reliable and professional service for travelers in need of door-to-door transportation. Taxis can be hailed on the street or booked in advance by phone, with fares calculated based on distance traveled and time spent in transit. Taxis are readily available throughout the city center and can also be found at taxi stands located at key transportation hubs, hotels, and popular tourist attractions.

Rental Cars:

Car Rental Agencies:
For travelers who prefer the flexibility and independence of driving, several car rental agencies operate in Rennes, offering a variety of vehicles for rent at competitive rates. Rental cars can be picked up and dropped off at designated locations throughout the city, including the train station and the airport. Visitors must have a valid driver's license and be at least 21 years old to rent a car in France, and international drivers may need to obtain an International

Driving Permit depending on their country of origin.

Walking:

Rennes is a pedestrian-friendly city with a compact city center that is easily navigable on foot. Many of the city's main attractions, shops, restaurants, and cultural landmarks are located within walking distance of each other, making it convenient to explore the city on foot. Pedestrian zones and sidewalks are well-maintained and well-marked, and the city's flat terrain makes walking an enjoyable and accessible way to get around.

In conclusion, Rennes offers a variety of transportation options for getting around the city and its surrounding areas, including public transit, bicycles, taxis, rental cars, and walking. Whether you're commuting to work, exploring the city's attractions, or venturing out into the countryside, Rennes' efficient and accessible transportation network ensures that travelers can navigate the city with ease and convenience.

Safety Tips and Emergency Contacts

Ensuring safety while traveling is paramount, and being informed about safety tips and emergency contacts can help visitors enjoy their time in Rennes with peace of mind. Here's a detailed guide:

Safety Tips:

1. Stay Aware of Your Surroundings: Remain vigilant and aware of your surroundings, especially in crowded areas,

tourist attractions, and public transportation hubs.

2. Keep Valuables Secure: Avoid displaying expensive items such as jewelry, cameras, and electronics in public. Keep valuables secure in a hotel safe or hidden pockets.

3. Use Licensed Taxis: When using taxis, ensure they are licensed and use reputable companies. Avoid accepting rides from unmarked vehicles.

4. Avoid Dark and Isolated Areas: Stay in well-lit and populated areas, especially at night. Avoid walking alone in dark or isolated areas.

5. Follow Traffic Laws: When walking or cycling, obey traffic laws and signals. Use

designated crosswalks and pedestrian paths.

6. Beware of Pickpockets: Keep wallets, purses, and bags secured and close to your body. Be cautious of crowded areas where pickpockets may operate.

7. Stay Hydrated and Sun Protected: During warmer months, stay hydrated and protect yourself from the sun by wearing sunscreen, a hat, and lightweight clothing.

8. Respect Local Customs and Laws: Familiarize yourself with local customs and laws to avoid unintentionally offending or violating regulations.

9. Emergency Preparedness: Carry a charged mobile phone with emergency

contacts programmed, as well as a list of local emergency numbers and addresses.

Emergency Contacts:

1. Police (Emergency): Dial 17 to reach the police in case of emergencies, including accidents, theft, or suspicious activities.

2. Fire Department (Emergency): Dial 18 in case of fire emergencies, including building fires, wildfires, or hazardous material incidents.

3. Medical Emergencies (SAMU): Dial 15 for medical emergencies, including accidents, injuries, and sudden illnesses. SAMU provides ambulance services and medical assistance.

4. European Emergency Number (112): Dial 112 for any emergency situation. This number provides access to police, fire, medical, and other emergency services.

5. Tourist Police: If you're a tourist and need assistance, contact the Tourist Police at +33 1 45 50 34 60. They can provide guidance and support in multiple languages.

6. Embassy or Consulate: If you're a foreign national and require assistance from your country's embassy or consulate, locate their contact information in advance.

7. Poison Control Center: In case of poisoning or chemical exposure, contact the Poison Control Center at +33 1 40 05 48 48 for assistance.

8. Roadside Assistance: If you experience car trouble or need roadside assistance, contact a local service provider or your rental car company for assistance.

9. Lost or Stolen Documents: If your passport, ID, or other important documents are lost or stolen, report it to the nearest police station and your country's embassy or consulate.

By staying informed, following safety precautions, and knowing who to contact in case of emergencies, visitors to Rennes can enjoy a safe and memorable experience in this charming city.

Conclusion

Final Thoughts on Rennes

Rennes offers visitors a rich tapestry of history, culture, and charm. From its medieval architecture and cobblestone streets to its lively cultural scene and gastronomic delights, Rennes is a destination that captivates the imagination and leaves a lasting impression on all who visit. As we conclude our exploration of this vibrant city, let's reflect on some final thoughts about Rennes:

Historical Heritage:

Rennes' rich history is evident at every turn, with its well-preserved medieval buildings, grand squares, and historic landmarks serving as a testament to its past. From the majestic Parliament of Brittany to the iconic Place des Lices, Rennes' architectural heritage tells the story of centuries of political, cultural, and artistic evolution.

Cultural Dynamism:

Rennes' cultural scene is as diverse as it is dynamic, with a thriving arts community that encompasses music, theater, dance, and visual arts. From world-class museums and galleries to lively festivals and events, Rennes offers endless opportunities for cultural exploration and creative expression.

Gastronomic Delights:

Rennes' culinary scene is a feast for the senses, with its vibrant markets, gourmet restaurants, and traditional creperies showcasing the best of Breton cuisine. From savory galettes and fresh seafood to artisanal cheeses and decadent pastries,

Rennes' gastronomic delights are sure to tantalize the taste buds of even the most discerning foodies.

Natural Beauty:

Surrounded by picturesque countryside, lush forests, and rugged coastline, Rennes offers visitors ample opportunities to connect with nature and explore the great outdoors. Whether hiking through the enchanting Brocéliande Forest, cycling along the scenic Ille-et-Rance Canal, or picnicking on the banks of the Vilaine River, Rennes' natural beauty is truly awe-inspiring.

Warm Hospitality:

Above all, Rennes is a city known for its warm hospitality and welcoming spirit. From the friendly locals who greet visitors with a smile to the passionate artisans and entrepreneurs who share their craft with pride, Rennes is a place where visitors are made to feel like family from the moment they arrive.

In conclusion, Rennes is a city of contrasts and contradictions, where ancient traditions blend seamlessly with modern innovations, and where the past coexists harmoniously with the present. Whether exploring its historic landmarks, savoring its culinary delights, or immersing oneself in its vibrant cultural scene, Rennes offers visitors an unforgettable journey of discovery and delight. As we bid farewell to this enchanting city, may the memories of our time in Rennes linger long after we've departed, serving as a reminder of the beauty, diversity, and boundless possibilities that await those who dare to explore its streets and embrace its spirit.

Recap of Must-See Attractions and Activities

As we conclude our journey through Rennes, it's essential to recap the must-see attractions and activities that make this city a truly remarkable destination. From its historic landmarks and cultural institutions to its culinary delights and natural beauty, Rennes offers a wealth of experiences for visitors to enjoy. Here's a detailed recap of some of the must-see attractions and activities in Rennes:

1. Historic Landmarks:
  - Parliament of Brittany: Admire the stunning architecture of this historic building, which has served as the seat of Brittany's regional government since the 17th century.

- Place des Lices: Explore the bustling market square, where vendors sell fresh produce, local specialties, and artisanal crafts every Saturday morning.

- Rennes Cathedral: Marvel at the intricate Gothic architecture of this majestic cathedral, which dates back to the 12th century and houses impressive stained glass windows and ornate chapels.

- Thabor Gardens: Escape the hustle and bustle of the city and wander through these picturesque gardens, featuring lush greenery, vibrant flowers, and tranquil ponds.

2. Cultural Institutions:

- Musée des Beaux-Arts: Discover a world-class collection of European art, including works by renowned artists such as Rubens, Delacroix, and Picasso, at this impressive museum.

- Les Champs Libres: Immerse yourself in culture and innovation at this multidisciplinary cultural center, which houses a library, museum, planetarium, and exhibition spaces.

- Opera de Rennes: Attend a performance at this elegant opera house, which showcases a diverse repertoire of opera, ballet, and classical music throughout the year.

3. Culinary Delights:

- Local Markets: Sample fresh produce, regional specialties, and artisanal products at one of Rennes' many local markets, such as the Marché des Lices or the Marché des Léopards.

- Creperies: Indulge in traditional Breton cuisine at a local creperie, where you can savor savory galettes and sweet crepes made with fresh, local ingredients.

- Cider Tasting: Experience the flavors of Brittany's famous cider at a local cidrerie, where you can sample a variety of apple and pear-based ciders paired with delicious Breton dishes.

4. Outdoor Adventures:

- Canal de l'Ille-et-Rance: Rent a bike or take a leisurely stroll along this scenic canal, which offers picturesque views of the countryside and charming villages along its banks.

- Bois de Coulanges: Explore this sprawling forest park on the outskirts of Rennes, where you can hike, bike, or picnic amidst ancient trees and winding trails.

- Vilaine River: Enjoy a leisurely boat cruise or kayak excursion along the tranquil waters of the Vilaine River, taking in the scenic beauty of the surrounding countryside.

5. Festivals and Events:

- Festival des Tombées de la Nuit: Experience the magic of this summer festival, which features outdoor performances, concerts, and street art installations throughout the city.

- Les Trans Musicales: Discover the next big thing in music at this renowned music festival, which showcases emerging artists and cutting-edge musical trends from around the world.

- Fête de la Musique: Join in the celebrations on World Music Day, as the streets of Rennes come alive with free concerts, performances, and festivities for music lovers of all ages.

In conclusion, Rennes is a city that offers something for everyone, from history buffs and art aficionados to foodies and outdoor enthusiasts. Whether exploring its historic landmarks, indulging in its culinary delights, or immersing oneself in its vibrant cultural scene, visitors to Rennes are sure to be captivated by the city's charm, beauty, and endless possibilities. So pack your bags, embark on your own adventure, and discover the magic of Rennes for yourself.

Farewell and Bon Voyage

As our journey through Rennes comes to an end, it's time to bid farewell to this enchanting city and reflect on the memories we've created during our time here. Rennes, with its rich history, vibrant culture, and warm hospitality, has undoubtedly left a lasting impression on all who have had the pleasure of exploring its streets and discovering its treasures.

Reflecting on Our Time in Rennes:

From strolling through the historic streets of the city center to savoring the flavors of Breton cuisine at local cafes and restaurants, our time in Rennes has been filled with unforgettable experiences and moments of wonder. We've marveled at the grandeur of the Parliament of Brittany, wandered through the picturesque Thabor Gardens, and immersed ourselves in the world-class collections of the Musée des Beaux-Arts.

We've delighted in the lively atmosphere of Place des Lices on market day, sampled fresh produce and artisanal goods at local markets, and indulged in the delicious creations of Rennes' talented chefs and bakers. We've explored the city's natural beauty along the banks of the Vilaine River, cycled through scenic countryside, and enjoyed leisurely boat cruises along the Canal de l'Ille-et-Rance.

We've celebrated the city's cultural diversity at festivals and events, danced the night away at Les Trans Musicales, and soaked up the magic of the Festival des Tombées de la Nuit. And through it all, we've been welcomed with open arms by the friendly locals, who have shared their stories, traditions, and way of life with us.

Farewell and Bon Voyage:

As we prepare to say goodbye to Rennes, let us carry with us the memories of our time here, as well as the lessons we've learned and the connections we've made along the way. May the spirit of Rennes continue to inspire us, wherever our travels may take us next, and may we always cherish the moments we've shared in this beautiful city.

Farewell, Rennes, and bon voyage! Until we meet again, may your streets be filled with laughter, your gardens with blooms, and your heart with the warmth of friendship and hospitality. Thank you for welcoming us into your embrace and for sharing your beauty, culture, and spirit with us. Au revoir, dear Rennes, and may our paths cross again someday.

Travel Planner

Destination (s)	When

Expenses	Budget	Actual

Transport ation		
Hotel		
Food		
Shopping		
Gifts		

Total		

Places to see

- _____

- _____

- _____

- _____

Places to eat

- _____

- _____

- _____

- _____

- _____

Places to shop

- _____
- _____
- _____
- _____
- _____

Emergency contacts

- _____

- _____

- _____

- _____

- _____

Addresses of places I'm staying at

- _____

- _____

- _____

- _____

125

Printed in Great Britain
by Amazon